Children's Book Illustration Guide for the Non-Traditional Creator

Four Techniques from a Crafter's Point of View

by Connie Dunn

Children's Book Illustration Guide by Connie Dunn, Copyright © 2013

Published by Nature Woman Wisdom Press

First Edition. Printed and bound in the United States of America.

All rights reserved. No part of this book may be reproduced in any form or by any electronic or mechanical means., including information storage and retrieval systems, recording, or photocopying, without permission in writing from the publisher, except by a reviewer, who may quote brief passages in review or where permitted by law.

Copyright © 2013 Connie Dunn

ISBN-13: 978-0615942360
SBN-10: 0615942369

9 8 7 6 5 4 3 2

Library of Congress

Dunn, Connie
    Children's Book Illustration Guide

Illustrations
    Children's Book Illustration Guide
    by Connie Dunn

Children's Book Illustrations
    Children's Book Illustration Guide
    by Connie Dunn

Table of Contents

Illustrations 5
Why Look for Options to Illustrate Your Book? 7
Book Design 11
The Art of Collage-Making for Children's Books....................23
Puppets – 3D creations and Backdrops 35
Quilts – Story Quilts 41
Designing in Felt and Fiber..53
Overview of My Journey in Art and Illustration.....................57
About Author 63

This is the cover of Momma Dee,
*an E-book collection of stories
available at www.uustoryteller.com*

Illustrations

Illustrations followed book printing history, since before the printing press there was not any need for illustrations. That's not to say that there was no art. Quite the contrary, before photography, portrait painting was very popular. Other paintings adorned the walls of homes, as well as tapestries. With the advent of the printing press, invented by Johannes Gutenburg in 1450, illustrations became as popular as the printed word.

The first illustrations were woodcut prints, which has had resurgence at different times throughout the more than 5 ½ centuries since printing was invented! With technology of the 21st Century, a lot more can be done. However, some books still lend themselves to many of the tried and true methods. While we can publish a book from our laptops, artwork can originate in other forms and be either scanned in or digitally photographed.

This Mermaid Picture Was Made
Through Foam Block Printing
A Method that Simulates
Wood Block Printing

There just about isn't any form of art that cannot be used for illustrating a book. In this book, we are focusing on Children's Book Illustrations, but this still leaves us a large variety of choices.

We probably all have seen and appreciated beautifully illustrated books done with oils or watercolors or even pastels. I have an acquaintance who has been illustrating children's books for many years. He's an accomplished artist. His paintings fall into that category of beautiful illustrations.

Not all books need beautiful pictures. Some books need silly pictures. Can you imagine *Cat in the Hat* illustrated with beautiful pictures? *Cat in the Hat* and other Dr. Seuss stories are not stories that would be improved by pretty pictures but pictures as outrageous and fun as the stories themselves.

I learned from an art teacher many years ago that children's books need to speak to the children. By looking into their art, we find what speaks to them. Their view of the world is not set into iconic shapes. Houses do not always have straight sides or absolute perspectives.

Caricatures and cartoons are often used. But there are many other things somewhere in between cartoon characters and beautiful paintings. This book will take you through four techniques that fall somewhere in that "in between" space.

These are techniques are not usually found in formal art programs. However, you can find everything you need for these projects at hobby and sewing stores.

Why Look for Options to Illustrate Your Book

Naturally, if you are a Children's Book Author, you will be thinking about illustrations for your book. If you choose a traditional publishing route, then this task will be done by the publisher. As an Independent Publisher, you stay in control of all pieces of the writing, publishing, and marketing processes. You choose what style your illustrations take. You choose and hire an illustrator or do it yourself.

Not everyone is comfortable creating art. However, if you are a creative person, then you might have some talents that you can use. Children's art is very primitive in nature. You can use some of those primal art techniques in your own creations, which takes some of the pressure off for making everything "perfect." Also, look at some modern artists, such as Matisse, then you can become more comfortable with the "imperfect." Henri Matisse was well-known for his use of color.

Henri Matisse Sample Pictures

Notice in these pictures that the bodies are not perfect. Matisse was heralded for his color expression over half a century, which earned him recognition as a leader in Modern Art.

Picasso was also a giant in the world of art. He, too, created rather "imperfect" paintings, if we gauge "perfect" by what we see as the human figure. However, art expresses far more than simply what we see in the "real" world. Art expresses emotion, movement, and often tells a story.

Pablo Picasso Sample Pictures

There are as many ways to do art as there are people. Do I totally get what Picasso and Matisse were trying to communicate? No, I'm not an art critic or art history aficionado. I know what I like, and I know what I don't like. I also know that when it comes to illustrating for children, you don't need to try too hard. In other words, you don't need to strive for some "perfection" that is in your head.

I have found that I'm not so good at drawing, but when it comes to fiber and fabric, I'm at home. Don't ask me why I can cut a piece of felt into a perfectly acceptable human form, but I feel I fail when it comes to drawing. All that really means is that drawing isn't my medium. I even found that paper works as a close second to fabric for me.

I think you have to try out different mediums to find your comfort level. Combine different mediums, such as paper and fabric or yarns and whatever. Add gel pens to the mix, which work well as a paint medium for both paper and fabric. However, fabric markers are more efficient on fabric.

My best medium is probably quilting, which is more like applique combined with some quilting. There are really no right or wrong ways to do art. I know a multi-media artist who makes these incredible three-dimensional scenes. She cuts out the same figures numerous times to create just the right three-dimensional affect. I doubt that I could do that, but it isn't my medium. It is my friend's medium.

Just like my friend who makes these great three-dimensional pictures, you need to explore to find what suits you. Not only does it need to be something you feel comfortable doing, you almost need to be passionate about it. You see, when you are illustrating a children's book, you will be creating a number of pictures. For a short book, maybe 20-25 pictures will be needed. For longer books, you may need to create twice that many. So you don't want to choose something that you think you can tolerate doing. If you have to create many different pictures, you need to be committed. Otherwise, you're better off hiring an artist to do the job.

I made a set of quilts for one book, but it was a collection of stories, which only required one quilt per story. For one story, you need more art, because you're creating a picture book. You need a picture on every page to illustrate the text on that page. You can get away with one page full of text when you have an illustration on the facing page.

Finding an Illustrator

If you don't feel confident enough to illustrate your book and you are either self-publishing or "indie" publishing, you might need to find an illustrator. You cannot turn to your local Yellow Pages and find an artist or illustrator. There are some listed on www.fiverr.com and www.elance.com, but they are mostly for one-shot graphics or logo creators.

High School and College art students are excellent choices to hire for a book illustration. Because the students have a small or no portfolio, ask them to do one picture before you make the decision to hire them. You need to fully explain what you want in the way of graphics to your illustrator, especially new artists. College art students often play with a lot of styles, so they may not have a "usual" style.

Even if you are hiring a graphics specialist, you need to ask the artists to create one picture, before you commission them for the entire book. The way that it works is you tell the artist each picture that you want to go into the book. It is often helpful to make a list of every piece of art that you want illustrated. In this way, the artist has an idea of what you want. It's also helpful when you do the illustrations yourself!

Book Design

Book Design includes everything from choosing your font to what your illustrations look like and where they are placed in your book. If you are a traditionally published author, this process is done by the publisher and you don't actually have any input. If you are an indie published author, you get to make all the choices, which could be scary if you didn't know what to do. After you read this section, you will hopefully be better informed to make better decisions. Relax! It's not as complicated as you might think!

Design Overview

There are some issues that you want to consider when you are designing your book. Think about how you want your book to look. If you aren't sure, then go to a library or book store and look at some of the books on the shelves.

Keep in mind what your skills are so that you stay grounded in what is doable rather than some dream that you don't have skills or money to invest to create. You can hire an independent book designer, but you have to know enough to talk with them. Otherwise your book might a direction you don't want. Keep in mind that whenever you release your creative control, anything can happen. It might be a good thing, but you have to remember that you need to communicate exactly how much control you wish to give the designer. So, be clear when you are working with professionals and either get testimonials or get them to do your first chapter before you hire them for the entire book.

Optimizing the design of your book for readability is an important design element. Most of us know that children's picture books have large print to make it easier for beginning readers. But if your audience is the elderly, you would need to design your book with large print, as well.

Understanding your target market will help you better understand how the design and readability factor will affect your potential buyers. If you want to be a spend-thrift and save money by creating a book in a small point size, then you might not sell many books, because people won't purchase something they cannot read. Children's Books, in particular, are usually printed with larger type to help young readers be able to read easier!

Larger print can even work to help illustrate the pages, as in the Dr. Seuss books. Some of the words are very bold and in different colors.

Audience

You need to please your audience or else your efforts are wasted. So, if you haven't figured out for which your audience your book will appeal to, then this is a good time to do think about it.

Discovering your audience takes some particular thinking. To say your book appeals to people of all ages and stages means that you have no clue for whom your book is written. We also need to understand that if your book is for more than one audience, there is usually a primary audience. For example, many folk tales have a primary audience of children and a secondary audience of adults. Often the audience can be broken down even more, such as male or female. Folk tales, in particular, can have a strong hero or heroine, which makes them more appealing to a particular gender,

We know that a text book is written for students; a fiction book for middle-school students is written for middle school students; and blogs and newsletters are written for customers or clients. Expanding on these obvious choices can help you figure out how to create a book for a specific audience.

Knowing who your readers are will help you write to their interests. This audience is your "target market." When the audience is too broad, it is more difficult to market to them. When the audience is more pin-pointed, you are able to reach them more easily. For example, if you chose everyone as an all-inclusive audience means that you have to divide your marketing budget into too many pieces. It's hard to find where "everyone" hangs out. But when you can narrow down the people who are most likely to be your readers, you more easily reach those people where they hang out on the Web, purchase newspapers or magazines, etc.

When you know the "audience," you know how to speak to them. When writing Children's Books, if you are writing for 3rd grade or 12th grade, you wouldn't use the same sentence structures or vocabulary. What you write would be different. Younger children need picture books, but high school students are more interested in more complex works ranging from fiction to non-fiction. So this would be the difference between *War and Peace* vs *The Lomax,* which is quite a difference. Therefore, you should better understand how "audience" affects everything about your book!

As you work on your "audience," start with who your potential readers are. Describe them in as much detail as you can. And naturally, with

Children's Books, you are not just creating a book for just the children, because it is all the adults that surround the children who are going to be buying the book. Therefore, the book has to appeal to the adults – parents, teachers, and grandparents.

Because this book is about illustrating Children's Books, we are narrowing down the market to "Picture Books," specifically. In so doing, we now can look closer to other parameters that can narrow the market:
- Age Level/Reading Level
- Fiction
- Non-Fiction
- Teaching Stories
    - Values
    - Religious
    - Educational
        - Math
        - Geography
        - History
        - Language
        - Art
        - Music
        - Etc.

Topic

Topics often dictate how we approach the book design. For example, if you are writing a non-fiction picture book about an historic event or person, we would approach the illustrations differently. We might be able to use actual photos or we might purposely use line drawings rather than color.

The topic of our Picture Book, you see, will make a difference how we want to not only illustrate the book but design it. Fonts might even help tell our story. If we choose Comic Sans, for example, the topic should be more fun than serious, because the font is more fun. It is more of a hand-printing typeface. However, if our book is serious, such as an historic event or person, then we might want a more serious typeface like Caslon or Arial, possibly even some of the serif typefaces, such as Palatino.

Explore different design elements for different topics. See what you like or don't like. Because you are in charge of book design, try out a variety in all areas. Try out things that you've never seen in a book or mimic one of your favorite Picture Book authors/illustrators.

Artistic Quality

Just about any book can be turned into a work of art, but some books lend themselves to it more than others. While you may think you aren't as artistic as you are good with words, remember that even words can become art.

If you think your book would be best illustrated with beautiful paintings, create beautiful paintings, use scenic photographs, or talk with local artists. Most communities have some sort of artistic community, an art gallery, an art school, community college with an art program. Explore options in your area; you might be able to collaborate with one of these artists.

In my small church community, there are quite a few artists – photographers and painters. Even though you are publishing as an indie author, you don't necessarily have to settle. Decide what you want and work toward that goal.

Personal Perspective

One of the strongest pieces of book designing is your personal perspective. It's YOUR book; and it's YOUR perspective! This is one of the most important REASONS that you probably decided to be an indie published author, so you can have total Creative Control!

Fonts & Typography

Readability figures into your font style. While fancy fonts may look interesting, if you cannot read them, then people will likely not purchase the book. Notice the covers of best sellers; they usually have large san serif type.

Notice the inside of books that you are reading or go to the library on a research journey to examine the typefaces in books. Notice what you like and compare that type with available types. You can do that by making a copy of the page and comparing the type with the typeface recommended by book designers.

The inside pages are either a sans serif or serif type and normally no smaller than 12 points. If your target readers have a disability, then you must adjust to their needs.

Fonts are only part of the design, but it is a huge piece of designing a book that is both pleasing, readable, and fits the needs of your marketing niche of readers. Typography is the design of fonts. It's a bit more than most independent or self-published book designers want to think about. However, you should have a working knowledge of the topic.

Cyrus Highsmith, author of Inside Paragraphs and professor of typography at University of Rhode Island, says "When I teach letter drawing, I have observed a similar phenomena. If the students can focus on drawing the empty space inside and around the letter, 90–95% of the issues of correct proportion, balance, and weight, get resolved. Then it is just a matter of making small refinements to the letters themselves."

In Highsmith's interview posted on www.fontfeed.com, he talks about how the font is no longer a printed book design issue. The font used has to look and be readable across print, e-readers, tablets, and cell phones. That's a lot of flexibility for something most of us never think about.

Highsmith continues: "When the pages change size, columns expand or contract, as the resolution goes up and down, the typography, what goes on inside paragraphs and beyond, needs to be carefully adjusted to suit the context." That's the reason that as an independent publisher, you need to appreciate typography, even if you only know what I have included here.

The Book Designer (www.bookdesigner.com) hosted blog written by Joel Friedlander on August 31, 2009, caught my eye. Friedlander, a self-published author says, "There's no bigger decision you make in designing a book than picking the body typeface."

"Any idiosyncrasy in the type design will be magnified by the repetition of typesetting 75,000 or 100,000 words in thousands of lines on hundreds of pages," Friedlander points out. There are five basic classic fonts that are recommended by book designers that make most books look great.

Five Classic Fonts

Garamond is known for its graceful, flowing style.

Janson is set apart by its strong thick and thin strokes.

Bembo has classic beauty. It is also liked for its readability.

Caslon is the classic font used in textbooks.

Electra has warm personality.

Profitability

In designing your book for profitability, you want to keep the page number count down. At the same time, you need to make it readable. There are ways to cut your costs, such as making the interior black and white rather than color. Even with Picture Books, black and white can work with a limited number of books; however, choose wisely. Color captures the imagination of children more often than not. The number of pages may not be as critical, because Picture Book Stories are usually short. However, most indie printer/publishers require a minimum of 24 pages.

Profitability, however, must be weighed with the overall salability as a product. If you are just cutting things out of your book to save money, you may find that you are just being too thrifty. Check out the book calculator on CreateSpace to see exactly how your choices fit into the cost of the book (https://www.createspace.com/Products/Book/#content6). To compare costs, go to LuLu's calculator (http://www.lulu.compublish/books/)

Where can you save in your design? The profitability of your book depends on the quality content of your book. If you've chosen a hardback book over a paperback, then you can probably save by creating your book as a paperback. NOTE: CreateSpace.com does not offer hardback books. Lulu.com does provide that as an option.

Perhaps you wanted elaborate paintings or graphics to go into your book, but the cost up-front is enormous. Be creative and choose another artist, which might be more affordable. One way to find a reasonable artist is to go to local high school or technical school and hire a student. Another option is to buy graphics or photos from a stock photo distributor, such as istockphoto.com and dreamstime.com.

Another way to cut costs is to choose a slightly larger trim size to cut down on the number of pages. You can also do your own illustrations, which is the purpose of this book.

Book Trim Sizes

Books come is some standard "trim" sizes. Trim refers to exactly what it says, trim! After a book is printed and bound, it often needs to be "trimmed" to the right size.

Some standard trim sizes are:
- 5-inches wide by 8-inches long
- 6-inches wide by 9-inches long
- 7-inches wide by 10-inches long

Laying Out Design Issues

In the olden days, which is only a few years ago, you would have to paste the text on your pages after they had been typeset. Pictures were also processed before being pasted onto your pages. In those days, you had everything separate and a blank canvass, so to speak, to fill.

You could visually see the page. The text and pictures had hot wax on the back, so you could just pick them up and then change it around, if you didn't like it. Now, everything is done inside the computer in your word processing software. If you want a border around each of your pages, you need to do that within the software, instead of manually pasting strips of tape with a variety of border choices.

If you want pictures to face a certain page, such as an illustration for a chapter, you need to format the pages in your word processing software to do that. Your act of formatting is what creates your Design within your word processing software. Formatting is actually the word we use for the actions of placing graphics, choosing fonts, paragraph breaks, etc. on the pages where you want them.

Once you have chosen the size of your finished book, which is called Trim Size, set a custom page size in your word processing software, which will automatically size the pages throughout your file.

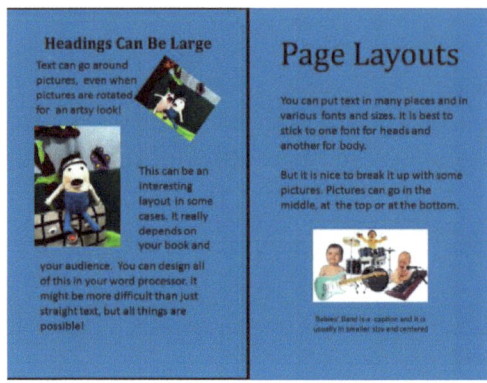

The most used size is 6-inch by 9-inch, which means 6-inches wide and 9-inches long.

Set a custom page size in your word processing software, which will automatically size the pages throughout your file. This is usually done by going into the Page Layout.

Once the trim size is set, then you have to go through each page and make sure everything is set the way you want it. Odd numbered pages are Right-Handed Pages, which is where we typically want Chapters to begin. Even numbered pages are the back sides or Left-Handed Pages. Placing a picture on the facing page or Left-Hand Page can be a good design option. However, in Picture Books, most designs include a picture on each page. Perhaps, you might have one page full of type with a picture on the facing page. However, picture book means just that: pictures!

Blank Pages need to be inserted to assure that Chapters begin on Right-Hand (odd numbered) Pages. With Picture Books, there are no Chapters. Once you have the Page Size chosen, I usually go into the View tab and set it to 2 pages. It will show you the Right-Hand Page and its back side or Left-Hand Page. In this way, I can easily format the page breaks or pagination

You can set the page up at the very start of your writing if you know what size you want your book to be. However, formatting will still need to be done after your writing is completed and all the editing has been done. Formatting page breaks will put the pagination in order. Books have page numbers, as well. While there are a number of ways to format these, there are some standard ways that books are done.

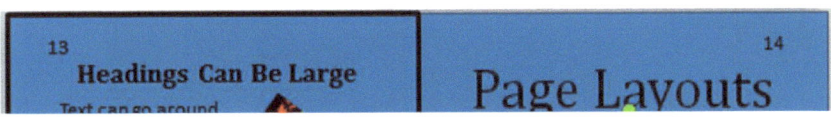

Page numbers and the Book Title are often placed in the margin above (header) or below (footer) the text. One way is to put the page numbers on the outside edges of the pages, this means that odd and even pages need to be formatted differently. NOTE: Microsoft Word (2010) makes it more difficult to make this work – not impossible but a little more difficult than in previous versions. Putting page numbers without the Title is a bit easier.

Page numbers can be centered on the page in either the header or the footer. You can center both the number and the title by putting the title in the header and the number in the footer. The page numbers and title are normally in a smaller font and are often italicized. I usually like to make them as small as 8 point. However, with Picture Books, a larger page number is used, as well as a larger font size for the text.

The Art of Collage-Making

What materials do you use when you do collage?

"Predominantly glossy magazine images, black and white and color, dark mat board, and matte medium as glue and sealer. Surgical scissors are good for cutting small details, long scissors for long straight edges, and I use a stubby brush," says Leah Goat, a collage artist, who lives in Hanover, New Hampshire.

Leah got into collage-making by taking a class at a local women's health center, she says. "The leader was a professional artist, so even though the class was therapeutic it also stressed aesthetics. I've also learned from *the Soul Collage* book and created *Soul Collage* cards." To be clear the *Soul Collage Cards* are a creation you make to gain insight into your own soul or inner landscape.

Soulcollage: An Intuitive Collage Process for Individuals and Groups by Seena B. Frost and *SoulCollage Evolving: An Intuitive Collage Process for Self-Discovery and Community* are recommended by Leah.

"Collage for me is meditation," explains Leah. "My collages arise from where I am, spiritually, psychologically, etc., at that moment. I go through many images rapidly, saving the ones that "speak" to me, combining

them in ways that touch me. This is an intuitive rather than an intellectual process. Sometimes it isn't until days later that I begin to see the meaning in what I've juxtaposed. I'm not sure how this would apply to illustration, where you have a pre-existing story line, unless your work was autobiographical."

Collages can be a spiritual experience; however, as illustrations, they are more of an artistic exploration of the text. Collages are fairly easy to make. You can use quite an array of items in collages, including wire, buttons, felt, paper of all different weights, gel pens, embroidery thread and just about anything else you can find.

Collages are usually constructed by cutting paper and gluing onto another paper. Collages by definition are mixed media creations. By using paper and paint, or paint and anything else, or any two or more mediums, collages are built. Collage comes from the French word "coller" meaning "glue."

In the collage on the previous page, a tree trunk was cut from printed zigzag pattern in brown. The green leaves were made from tissue paper. The dog and the cat were both made out of felt, thus a multi-media piece of art.

Glasses on the two "grandmas" were made from wire. The book title is: *Destiny's Two Grandmas: Why Do Things Change?"* The collaged pages are each unique and go with the text on each of the pages.

The design of this book has the pictures remaining on one page. They mostly take up a large space on each page. While some picture books have pictures that flow over both left and right pages with type going over elements in the picture. This is a fairly standard picture book illustration. However, having pictures free-standing on each page is also a design that you see a lot in picture books.

Before embarking on illustrating, you might look at other picture books to see how they are constructed and designed. You can emulate any that you prefer. However, when putting text over the art, you need to make sure that the text is still readable.

In layering tissue paper, it's possible to create the illusion of a crowd of people without creating details of each person.

In this manner, it appears as if the crowd were slightly blurred, which happens when you take pictures and blur the background making the subjects sharply in focus. This technique creates a similar effect.

The technique of collage is hundreds of years old and has its origin firmly rooted in the invention of paper in China, which happened around 200 BC. However, as an art form, the collage is attributed to both Georges Braque and Pablo Picasso in the early 1900s, even though some portrait painters before them used things like chains and gems glued to their portraits.

Picasso's "The Dream" below is one of Picasso's famous collages. It is available in a reprint on canvas. Notice how her face is split, yet clearly a face. This is a technique that Picasso used to create some drama. Notice that in the picture below, the body sort of flows without so much form with the exception of the face and hands.

Picasso's The Dream
Prints are available at
(http://www.icanvasart.com/pablo-picasso-dream-canvas-print.html)

Picasso and Braque created a genre of art called "Cubism," which essentially is collage. The picture below is a Braque's Violin and Newspaper. It illustrates how this artist combined mediums to create what is now considered a masterpiece!

Braque's Violin and Newspaper
Source:
http://www.philamuseum.org/collections/permanent/51170.html

Collage is very easy art to do and has the flexibility to be used by young children as well as adults. The materials are commonly found either to purchase or recycle. There are few rules in making a collage, as well.

Can you imagine how different this "Cubism" Collage art must have felt over a century ago when these two courageous artists embarked on this revolutionary modern art technique?

While they were obviously leaders in the art world, it is worth a look at what else was happening in the world at that time. During the four decades from 1870 to 1910, all sorts of new technology were invented...more than had happened in the previous four centuries!

Portrait painters were relegated to the back seat due to photography advancements. Other technological inventions included cinematography, sound recording, the telephone, the motor car and the airplane!

We have made other advancements during the last century: space flight, computers, cell phones and other digital devices. We now can read books on an electronic reader rather than turning the pages of a book. We even have interactive books. Movies and games are so portable they fit on our cell phones!

Illustrations will still be needed no matter if it's for digital or print. So we still need ways to create illustrations that capture the imagination of our audience – and Children's books, in particular, are heavily illustrated.

Typically, when we think of collages, we think of magazine cutouts glued on a piece of paper. The cutouts, of course, can be words or pictures or a combination of the two. The collage below takes Matisse's Icarus and adds other images over it. This collage was done on the computer, but follows the same ideas as cutting and pasting!

Torn tissue paper collages are a favorite activity of children around the winter holidays, because it simulates stained glass.

Combining ribbon; paper, especially homemade papers; portions of artwork; photos; three-dimensional items; found items, such as shells or stones; and other objects make collages fascinating.

One of my favorite *Famous Artists* was Henri Matisse. In the latter part of his life following a diagnosis of cancer and surgery, he began making cut outs, which by definition fall into the category of collage by gluing or adhering the cutouts to a canvas or paper.

Some of Matisse's cutouts were large, real-size pieces. My favorite is the Jazz Icarus pieces, in particular the blue background with a black cut out of a human figure.

In this series, Matisse chose not to be precise and so bodies were recognizable but misshapen. Notice in the picture on the preceding page; see how the body isn't precise? The body is dark placed on a lighter background with splashes of brighter color.

Matisse sparked art curriculum for K-12 that help children learn about color and shape. According to http://www.henri-matisse.net, Matisse would create his pieces over a period of time. He cut out pieces and left them pinned to a wall. They would tremble in the slightest breeze. The pinning of images to the wall began the second process. In this process, Matisse would then combine the images after they had proven interesting shapes.

Notice in the photo on the page above, how he had a sea of colored paper all around him. While no one actually spoke about this, I feel this picture so depicts the artistic process. We see his collage on the wall behind him.

Matisse called these "cut-outs", but I see them clearly as collage. It's interesting to note that Matisse used this art form almost exclusively near the end of his life. In fact by about the mid-19th-century, he used this method for such projects as wall hangings, tapestries, and scarf patterns.

Photo collages and software on computers now allow all sorts of collage-making. It's a new world of collage going into the 21st Century.

The collage above was made on the computer, using a Matisse cut out art piece as the base for the collage.

Whether collages are done on paper or canvas or on the computer, they make remarkable artwork.

Collages offer flexibility for a wide variety of options. You can cut out shapes, layer different textures, use newspapers, magazines, old calendars, etc. for words or graphics to add to your collage.

Trying your hand at collage is easy. While scrapbooking has become a huge industry, it offers a lot of raw materials. Scrapbooking by definition of collage fits into the classic collage. As with most art, you have to have some idea of what you want to do. Collages can make good cover art, as well.

Whether you are cutting out large pieces or using a bunch of smaller pieces, creating a collage is somewhat like putting together a puzzle - only you are creating the pieces and still have to figure out where those bits fit together.

The Academy of Art University in San Francisco has a whole school devoted to illustration. They tout it as a *visionary storyteller*. I like that name, I think it speaks well to the collage and perhaps other mediums, as well. The collage they use in their marketing is alluring, as well.

If you are new at illustrating children's books, I suggest giving a try to making a collage. There aren't any major obstacles to jump over. It's a relatively inexpensive endeavor. Cut out shapes, cut out words or letters, and put them all together.

Experimenting with collage making is really quite fun. What to use?
Use These in Collages:
- Torn paper;
- Cut out or die cut paper;
- Wax and embossing;
- Glitter, sequins, crystals, etc.;
- 3-D items, found or purchased;
- Gems, pearls, or beads;
- Paint, or puffy paint;
- Ribbons, rickrack, fringe, and other trims;
- Buttons, etc.

The backdrop here was made from two pieces of felt sewn together: the blue and green, then the tree was cut and stuck onto the felt backdrop. Other things, like the leaves and butterflies, were also cut from felt and stuck onto the felt backdrop.

Notice that since the objects are in front of the backdrop, they, too, must sit on something like a mini-stage. In this case, a lighter green felt.

Puppets – 3D creations and Backdrops

It is with great pleasure that I present this section. I believe it is unique to illustrate with puppets. Because puppet illustrations are rare, it only means that the book will stand out.

Puppets are always fun. It really allows you to make your character(s) come alive. Features can be completely customized, such as the addition of glasses, shown in the picture below. This puppet was further customized with the addition of sagging cheeks and lots of wrinkles to match the elderly person that she is. I affectionately call her, Miss Odell, my mother's name. She wears a wig from my mother and a pair of glasses that she gave me. She vaguely resembles what my mother looked like. I accentuated the wrinkles and the jowls, which my mother didn't have.

The biggest drawback to using puppets as illustrations is that it takes time to create them. As with the "Dumpty" family (below), I not only had to sew them, I had to create a pattern. Fortunately, eggs aren't too difficult!

I also created finger puppet patterns for the Dumpty Family, which were put into the book, as well. Children love finger puppets. These were simple patterns so that even moms who weren't real crafty could easily create them.

No sewing is needed, you can glue it all! Sewing works just as well, of course!

Puppets are not a medium that is typically used in illustrations for books. Current memory would bring up many uses in stage and parade usage. It may be surprising to note that puppets have their origin – no not with the Muppets – in India almost a thousand years B.C.

The first puppets were stick puppets, which were used to tell the ancient stories of Maha-Bharata and Bala-Ramayana. Japanese and Indonesia had similar puppetry origins.

Puppetry flourished in Italy in the 18th Century. In the 19th Century Vaudeville was hugely popular, but a marionette theater gave them a run for their money.

Then, in the 20th Century, enter the Muppets! Who couldn't love Big Bird or Oscar, the Grouch? The eternal love story with Kermit, the Frog, and Miss Piggy, has to bring a smile to everyone's face!

While Jim Henson is no longer here to keep evolving the Muppets, his team has carried that on for him. And the thing is that the history of puppetry doesn't end here. It is an on-going art form. It has been here for thousands of years and will likely be here for another thousand.

As a medium for children's book illustration, puppets may be a bit ground breaking. I'm fairly sure that it won't stay that way. I admit, however that using puppets takes some time and investment. Depending on what cast of characters you have, you'll need to create a unique puppet for each character in the story. Then, there is the background or set!

Making puppets is a fun hobby for me. However, creating a huge cast for a book can be daunting. Even creating unique clothing items helps add that customization that is required when these pieces are illustrations.

I first got into making puppets after finding patterns for "big mouth" puppets. These puppets were large "stage" size puppets…26-inch tall.

The puppets below are four of my puppets. For the green puppet, I used a green wig left over from Halloween. His glasses are unique, as well. Whenever I am out shopping, I purchase interesting items. These little glasses were probably from the Dollar store. They were like plastic tubing bent into glasses.

The patterns were purchased on the Internet from http://www.puppetpatterns.com/ people_puppet.htm. Mixing up colors for the puppets gives a multicultural feel to the collection.

I basically start in the center of the head and go around, leaving sort of a part down the center of the head.

In this case, the yarn hair was pulled into pigtails and tied with the same yarn. Then ribbon tied over that.

The pink puppet next to the green puppet has yarn hair. The hair is sewn in one strand at a time. I cut long strands of yarn about twice the finished length of the hair. Using a needle, the yarn is pulled through the fabric. I pull it half-way through and tie it at the scalp.

The yellow puppet also has a wig. The best time to buy wigs is after Halloween when they are on sale. The fourth puppet on the very edge of the picture also has a wig. She also has a sparkly pink hat on. The wig is pulled into a ponytail through the back of the hat.

All the clothing is purchased in the kids' department. I sometimes take the puppets with me to try the clothes on the puppets. They wear toddler size clothes. If the bottoms are stretchy, I usually get a 2T or 3T. They are always too long. Tops and dresses can be 3T or 4T.

Shoes are usually size 4 or 5. Again, having the puppet with you helps when fitting clothing items on the puppet.

There are different sorts of puppets to make. The above right picture is of a puppet made from a pattern called a "glorified sock" pattern (http://www.projectpuppet.com/servlet/-strse-1/simple-sock-puppet-pattern/Detail). The pattern is basically a hand puppet that resembles a sock with a more fully developed head, working mouth and arms.

Then you can modify and embellish, which is what I did on the above. Her eyes stand out, because her eyelashes are rainbow colored with a bit of sparkle. They were purchased after Halloween, as well. I find a lot of items marked to 75% off after Halloween!

The cover below shows another book that is illustrated using puppets.

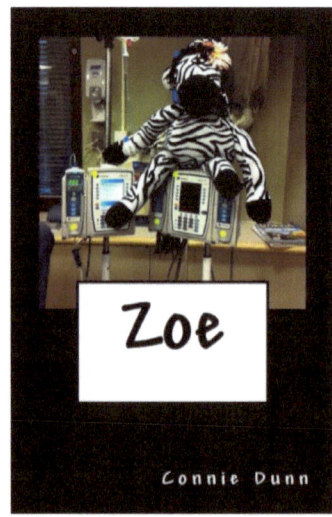

Quilts – Story Quilts

Story quilts are small artful quilts. These have been my newest discovery. They have similarities to collages. Most of all *Story Quilts* depict a scene out of the story. Some are more of a collage of different scenes.

Using the term "quilt" might actually be an exaggeration. However, I attended a workshop for "Fabric Art" where we made small artful quilts. The techniques were fairly simple in nature and more complex in execution.

The techniques that I learned in the workshop were valuable. Learning how to appropriately use the iron-on fusion, sometimes called "Wonder Under" was certainly a revelation. I had always ironed it on the wrong side of the fabric that I wanted to use, and then cut out the shape.

The technique that I learned was to iron it onto the backside, but instead of cutting it out with the paper on the back, remove the paper backing. Then, cut out the shape.

While these may seem like small details, they actually make a difference in building your quilt. Our instructor also taught us to iron on the fusion to the back of the fabric that is our background fabric. Remove the paper. Iron the fabric onto the batting. Using parchment paper, you can keep the fusing glue from getting on your iron.

Before sewing anything, place everything on the background fabric – after having put the fusion on all the fabric pieces removing the paper backing then cutting out the shapes – when you are set with how it looks, place the parchment over the pieces and iron them on.

Sewing comes next. There are several techniques for sewing.

First, you'll want to put the back fabric behind the batting. This piece will not be seen, since the small quilts are meant for hanging on a wall as a decoration.

You can quilt on a grid, which means that you make straight line stitching at the same interval over the entire quilt. You use a regular foot on the sewing machine or a "walking" foot, which helps keep all the fabric together.

An alternative method is to use zigzag stitches for sewing down some pieces or around the edges of all the pieces.

Sewing inside pieces or around the rest of the fabric outside of the design using the freehand foot on the sewing machine adds dimension. It means that you move the fabric around under the needle. It takes a bit to get the hang of it, but after a while it feels pretty natural.

When creating the scenes, designs, whatever it is you are creating, using different fabrics can change the feel of the entire quilt. For example, the trees pictured above were cut out of a plaid material and quilted with green thread gives you the illusion of leaves.

I also use embroidery to add details to my pictures. In the quilt pictured on the left, the leaves are embroidered. The tree is brown felt. And in keeping with fun children's art, I often put a sun shining in the window alongside the tree that is almost always placed where it can be seen.

Just to make sure that when you think of *quilt*, we're all on the same page. A quilt is defined as "the stitching together of fabric and padding."

Typically, a quilt has a top that is pieced together and is the design part of the quilt. Then, there is the batting, which is usually cotton, and finally, a backing fabric, which is often solid.

While we typically think of quilts being an American pioneer original, quilting is much older than that. It originates in ancient Egypt. Quilt making dates back to the 12th Century. Pieced linen rugs may also have been part of our ancient history. One example sits in a Russian Museum, which was found in a Mongolia Cave.

Quilt making was something that girls learned from their mothers. I learned from mine and my grandmother. My first quilt was a Nine-Patch quilt, which is basically three squares across and three down. Strips are then sewn to connect the squares. My mother and grandmother quilted it. Big quilts are very difficult to make, because of their size. You make the top first and then attach the batting and backing material, quilt and bind. But because it is such a large pieced fabric, you need a large quilting frame.

In older times, the quilting was done as a community project, which made quick work of a large project. Smaller quilts are more workable. The small artful quilts are definitely more doable. They fit in your lap and can easily be quilted on a regular sewing machine. However, with all the great quilting machines available, if you're going to do a lot of quilts, a quilting machine would be a great investment.

I like hand sewing over machine sewing for some pieces of my quilt making. I like the fine stiches that I can do by hand over the zigzag pattern. However, I also find that fabrics that ravel are best done with zigzag over the edges. Other fabric, such as felt or fleece, is often better with hand stitching.

It is probably a personal preference that you'll need to make for yourself. Quilts are no longer just a bunch of tiny pieces sewn together in geometric shapes. I've seen some fantastic quilts that are very artful and beautiful. One of my fellow students created a gorgeous mermaid.

I'm just beginning to work on another book and want to make my quilting more beautiful than the story quilts. The concepts in the book are more abstract, such as Mother Earth and God, so the quilts will need to feel more spiritual and ethereal than the quilts I've already created. This is a single story instead of a collection, which changed the parameters.

There is such a strong connection of weaving stories and weaving tapestries, which is another word sometimes used to describe quilting. Technically, a tapestry is woven on a loom. Quilts are pieced together from a combination of fabrics. During the quilting process, they are often stretched on a loom-like contraption that is similar to embroidery hoops only bigger and more rectangular.

It's the details that you can add to artful quilts that makes the difference. For example, on the quilt on the previous page, notice that she has on a sports jersey, a football under his arm, and there are several other sports balls on the quilt. The soccer ball can be seen in this photo.

In contrast, in this picture, we see her friend blinged out with rhinestones. The cat pictured here is made of felt and fabric marker. Instead of yarn hair on this character, she has felt hair with a big bow and more bling!

There really are no real limitations when making a quilt. I've used three-dimensional items on some of the quilts. These features add depth to an otherwise two-dimensional creation.

In the above picture, notice how the moccasins and the ballet slippers are three dimensional. I actually fashioned these out of felt. In fact, the backpack was also created with all its parts then sewn onto the back of this character.

These buttons and beads add some three-dimensional flavor, but more than anything, they offer familiar items for a bedroom. These add a bit of fun-factor to the quilt.

One of the important few words of wisdom that I can share with you is that details help make the story quilts interesting for the children. At first glance, they might not seem like much to add. However, these small details make the quilts more interesting. As a mom, I remember pointing out things for my daughters to name when they were small. They're all grown up now! I suppose that I have not grown up, because I still like creating stories and art.

There are many other ways to create a story quilt than the ways that I have mentioned here. Getting books at your local sewing or craft store will give you more details.

Designing in Felt and Fiber

Cutting felt is fairly easy. You really only need a nice sharp pair of scissors and a stack of colorful felt squares...they are called felt squares, but they are actually rectangular 9-inch by 12-inch. For a variety, add in some of the newer printed felt choices.

In the picture below, I used a dark color of felt as the base of my picture. With felt, you don't really need to sew or glue it down, because it all sticks nicely together. You may remember the old felt or boards from preschool. This is the same theory!

Chocolate Chip Cookies

In this collection of illustrations, I only used felt. I didn't use any embroidery thread. I did, however, use my gel pens. If you notice on the right side of this picture there are cookies that look like chocolate chip cookies.

The dots on the cookies are done with a gel pen. A permanent marker can also be used. What I liked about using the gel is that it tended to smear less.

Expressions on faces are harder to do in felt, simply because of the smallness of the canvas for which you are working. Small pieces of felt for eyes and mouths are more smile-oriented, especially since we are depicting children. The more details you put in, the older the face looks.

You shouldn't be concerned about making everything "perfect." The charm of children's art is that it isn't! Naturally, there are those illustrators that do tend to be more detailed and more "perfect" in their art creations. But in the world of children's literature and its art, there is a wide array of artistic representation.

In the illustration below, one character has oversized hair. The hair is part of the character development. Notice, also that I used tiny pieces of brown felt for bird seed.

Sometimes the pictures can aid the story. At other times, the pictures simply follow the storyline.

The beauty of using felt is that you can use pieces over and over. There's no need to keep the pictures intact, which gives you some flexibility in creating the remainder of the pieces.

Dragon Puppet

Overview of My Journey in Art and Illustration

I began my journey of illustrating my own children's books when I began taking art classes from a local art teacher. I learned how to sketch by looking at the lines rather than an overall piece. Instead of drawing from what we generally have believed a shape should be, we make it abstract and draw the lines, as we see them.

Our art teacher asked each of us why we were in the class. I told her that I wanted to illustrate children's books – my own stories.

I may have been in my third round of classes, when my instructor told me that I shouldn't take any more classes. She felt that I was at just the right place for illustrating children's books.

This drawing was made on the computer.

I wondered, of course, if I was really just a hopeless case or if she really felt that I could illustrate. The trouble was that I had no confidence in my own abilities.

She said that drawing just needed practice. I still practice sketching every now and then, but I do more on the computer. It has taken time to be happy with the results, and I believe that I'm a better fiber and fabric artist!

A Whale Sporting a Backpack Drawn for
The Fairies of Ferry Beach

One of my first books to illustrate was *The Most Magical, Awesome, Delicate Creature of All.* This was a new myth about how butterflies came to be, so the book was mostly butterflies.

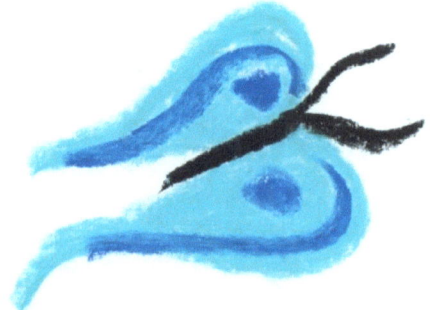

Butterfly made with Pastel Chalk for the book,
"The Most Magical, Awesome, Delicate Creature of All"

I used pastel chalk to illustrate all the pictures in this book. The hardest part was not creating the art, but trying to keep the chalk from smudging. I ended up putting each page into a plastic protective sheet. Then, I could scan them.

When I decided to write a new Humpty Dumpty story, I chose to make puppets. *The Real Story of the Dumpty Family* has a new character, *Mrs. Dumpty*, who knows exactly how to fix Humpty Dumpty, even though all the King's men and all the King's horses couldn't help.

All of the characters, including the Wall, were puppets. They also needed the appropriate backdrop. Felt pieces to make the sky and earth (blue and green) were sewed together. The felt backdrop was then hung on a wall, creating a very large felt board. The tree and butterflies were stuck onto the felt.

With many of my books, I've created drawings on my computer. I first learned this skill when working as a technical writer. I did not realize that

I would be called upon to draw anything. After all, I was a technical writer not a technical artist.

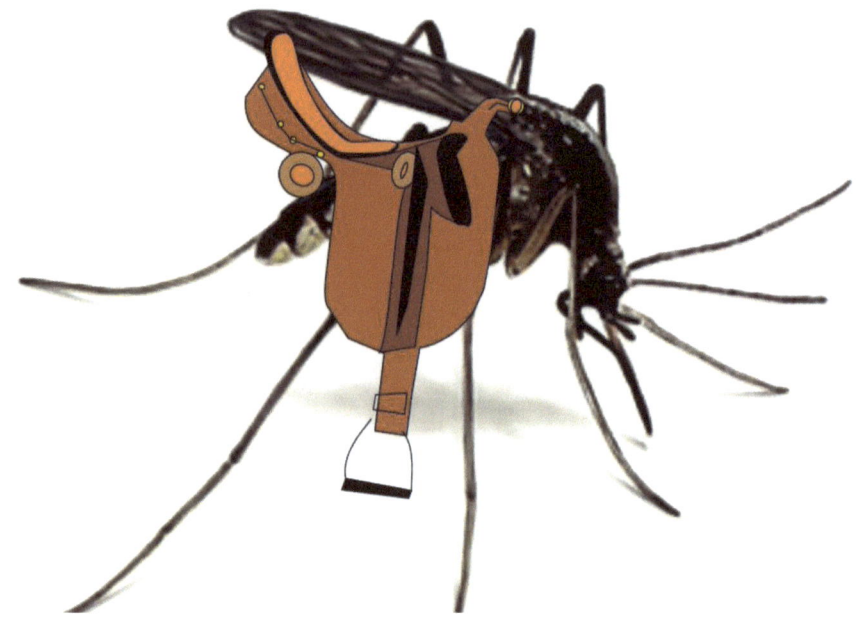

Mosquito Wearing a Saddle Illustrates the Story
Auntie Twit and the Texas Mosquitoes
published in The Fairies of Ferry Beach

This job happened to have me working on-site rather than freelance off-site, which was handy. I had no experience in creating technical graphics. There was one person in the office that was supposed to be in charge of drawing everything. However, that was rather a tall order and didn't happen that way. Instead, she showed me how to draw in CorelDraw™.

That gift of learning CorelDraw™ has allowed me to draw a lot of different graphics. One easy way to create a unique drawing is to bring a picture into CorelDraw™, then redraw on top of the drawing using the nodes to create the shapes into what you want. Once you've got some of the basic shapes, you can delete the original picture and finish the drawing as you prefer.

The picture below is a combination of computer graphics and photography. I would not have thought to do this without a little inspiration. I read about how an illustrator created her art originating with a photo. She turned the photo into a cartoon. If I have that capability, then I don't know how to access it, but it gave me the idea of placing my aliens into a photo.

This is the Cover Photo for The Aliens Among Us, *a book full of very short, short stories and scheduled for publication in February or March, 2014*

I'm the official logo & storytelling puppet at Ugly Dog Books

About Connie Dunn

Connie Dunn is an author, speaker, educator and owner of Publish with Connie and Nature Woman Wisdom Press. She writes courses, such as her signature, "12 Easy Steps to Publishing," children's books, such as her collection of children's stories, "A Spider, Some Thread, and a Labyrinth Walk," and non-fiction, such as "Press Releases Made Easy."

She has more than 25 years of experience in writing for magazines and newspapers. She had a regular column in the Dallas Morning News, which focused on small and home-based businesses. For this column, she won an award from the SBA (Small Business Administration). Connie also developed courseware for a number of start-up technology firms.

She worked with publishers, such as Prentice Hall and Taylor Publishing as a Developmental (content) Editor. She self-published her first book in 1981, and developed a collection of stories with a collaborator in the 1990s.

She writes children's books, non-fiction, and fiction. Connie believes that everyone has a book in them and her greatest joy is in traveling with her students on their writing journeys.

Connie is also a crafter and seamstress. She says, "I'm more comfortable with making things in 3D than I am with drawing. I can't draw, but I can cut out a figure much easier!"

THE END

www.ingramcontent.com/pod-product-compliance
Lightning Source LLC
Chambersburg PA
CBHW042002150426
43194CB00002B/102